DEAR JACK

Also by Jill Stengel

equinox (Dusie, 2011)
and I would open (Ypolita, 2011)
only this (Dusie, 2010)
lagniappe (Dusie and Nous-Zot Press, 2008)
may(be) (Dusie, 2007)
late may (Dusie, 2006)
ladies with babies (Boog City, 2003)
History, Possibilities : (a+bend press, 1999)
cartography (WOOD, 1999)

DEAR JACK

Jill Stengel

BLACK RADISH BOOKS
www.blackradishbooks.wordpress.com

Thank you to the following editors for publishing selections from *Dear Jack*: Reb Livingston, *No Tell Motel*, www.notellmotel.org, 2007; Mark Young, *Otoliths*, www.the-otolith.blogspot.com, as part of a special feature curated by Eileen R. Tabios, issue 17, 2010; and David Kirschenbaum and Buck Downs, *Boog City,* issue 74, 2012.

Many and varied thanks go to Abigail Albrecht, Andy Hilliard, Chuck Stebelton, Dana Teen Lomax, David Kirschenbaum, David McIntire, Jamen Howe, Jill Koetke Thompson, Mark Lamoureaux, Mark Pitts, Nicole Mauro, Niels Cappel, Susana Gardner, and the women of the Poet-Moms listserv.

These poems were originally written from December 1999 through Spring 2000.

Cover design by Susana Gardner
Author photo by Mark Pitts

First printing 2013 in the United States of America

ISBN: 9780985083700
LCCN: 2012913380

dear jack,

after falling. missing years. a memory somewhere.
locket, a picture.

fingerprints on fingertips.

can't find you—can't find you—then found you.

warmth.

an airplane takes you away.

I am left with: writing paper, a pen.
what I started with.

with love.
Jill

dear jack.

the blood beneath the band-aid.

I was safe.

jill

dear jack.

what night brings morning erases.

this is not always truth.

afar,
jill

we are always strangers, all of us.
knowing and forgetting, relearning ourselves
and the world, and the ways in which
we come together.

a moment. an opening. iris, dilating.

again.

dear jack.

want does not always equal have.
desire has many components.

all of this flying and leaving.
all of this staying.

j.

how can a voice caress

a fine dust.
and nothing to say.

J

Tarnish.
Unripen.

Which way.

reflections.
what shimmers.

dear j—

there is a myth.
I am dead.
it is a story
to be untold.
                    Jillian

generative.

what is this.

so there you have it, Jack…

my desire and my withholding.

what I can and cannot give.

dear Jack—

scintillating possibilities.

a match.

strike a match.

Jill

dear Jack—

the words keep coming. as do the pictures.
real and imagined.

soon distinctions will blur.

they float.

with love—
Jill

Dear Jack—

I rub my eyes   open to still paper
then close them   still pen

—J

dear—

of course you're not jack.
why would you be.

jill—

Dear Jack.

I could spend the rest
of my life without
ever seeing your face
again.

you
have other options.

you
have undeveloped film.

I
have only hands,
eyes

open

Dear Jack

Dear Jack

Dear Jack

Dear Jack

Dear Jack

I write to you in my
	little french notebook
when all the world's
	asleep

Jack—

you are fading

your emulsion

thins

J—

what am I going to
do with you when
you are done—

what is most amazing
is how the ordinary
of life keeps on
after the wondrous occurs

Dear Jack—

a point in a line of points

a star in a sky of stars

which one is you

do you shimmer
                    for me

Dear Jack—

last night I wanted
    to kiss you

last night I imagined
    kissing you

last night I thought

A range   not of mountains

Falling and climbing everywhere

Dear J—

I waited.
I waited and waited.
I waited and waited and
waited and waited and
waited and waited and
waited.

Jill

Dear J—

Patience was never one of
my virtues.

I tried it on for you.

It never did fit properly.

Only so many alterations one
can make till fabric falls apart.

—J

Dear Jack

today I spoke with you
as if we were having
a conversation

we were witty

I strike small keys
with the letters of your
name
          my fingers filling
for a moment the little
indentations

I have no reason to think
of you this way

I cannot help myself

Dear Jack

How old were you when you
learned to read?
To write?
Was it easy,
to write,
when you first began?
The clumsy pencil. Big
letters on grey-beige paper.
Blue lines, solid and dashed.

When I learned cursive,
the letter most difficult—
the capital J.

I drew her backward.

This is a true story.

J

Dear Jack—

I want to write you
big long poems, love
poems or other sorts
of poems, poems with
meaning, poems with importance,
poems with something to say.

Instead, I think
of you and I'm all-
a-jitter and the method
of expression I'm most
familiar with falls away
into fits, starts, sputters and worse.

As so often happens
with you, I am left
with nothing.

Jill

Dear Jack—

what is a stolen moment
where is it stolen from
or from whom

did you take my time
from me?

          what
have you done with my
time,
          my heart—

J

Dear Jack

Remembering
and that's where things
get cloudy. Certain
stories won't match,
I won't ask for your
version.
        How could I?

J

Dear Jack—

How many Jacks in a deck
Jokers, Queens and
Kings alike—

One-eyed Jack, suicide
King, which Queen
am I?

Dear Jack—

You never knew your
own value.
          Then again,
neither did I.

Dear Jack—

I am running out of things
to say to you.

J

Dear Jack—

A gulf, and throwing
rope or something
to the other side

How many times
How many times

before the rope
recoiled   departs

J

Dear Jack—

There are no poems
for your skin

There are no poems
for your eyes

There are no poems
for your lips

There are no poems
for your body, your
beauty, your grace
and all—

There are no poems
for you my Jack

These poems are
all for me.

Dear Jack—

The light in the room
and your movements

certain I missed a beat

pretending everything
the same nothing amiss

except my heart like dust
motes scattered in the sun-filled room

J

Dear Jack—

The faces you wear

J

Dear Jack—

Or someone else. Or
someone else.

Dear Jack—

you are what I make you

Dear Jack,

I can draw your
face but never from
memory

Dear Jack—

should there be air
on the other side

and how to breathe it

J

Dear Jack

If you thought you
were special

you were

Dear Jack—

There are many billions of bodies
and souls. Right this very now.

What do you say to that idea
of only one partner, perfect—

the soul-mate idea. A puzzle with
no boxtop to follow. Haystack, needle.

Snowflakes are now known to be
not each one unique. Social Security

numbers multiply assigned.
What of my thumb-print,

my soul-print—what if we
have no souls? There may be

three, seven, one hundred twelve
people at this instant with whom

I—or you—could build a life
of sorts—some kind of life.

-J-

Dear Jack—

when I think of your blond brown
red grey black absent hair

how it looks when it's dyed
some bizarre color when the
wind blows when you're
freshly awakened when your
hat comes off your head
when you've polished it—

oh Jack.
when I think of you
I lose all sense.

J

Jack—

when I think of you I
lose everything.

J

Dear Jack—

Cornish game hens with little socks.
West or White Castle burgers.
Blowfish.
Frog.
Emu.

Some things I never ate with you.
Likely never will.

Jill

Dear Jack

I want

I try

I cannot

Dear Jack—

O, to bottle you,
dispense you at will

It would never work, of course
but what are my other options

Dear Jack—

The conversation
never ends—

Jill

Dear Jack—

I have moments saved
like snapshots, pieces

good news
bad news

I see you again and again,
those moments—

J

oh forgive
we all must forgive

fools on fools' journeys
stumbling

dear jack—

I have every letter you ever sent me

I think

Jill

dear jack—

jack is not jack

dear jack—

who are you?
I want to touch you

J

Dear Jack—

and now I see you
in my dreams, in my books,
in my face, in my clothes,
in my haircut, in my
smile, in my furniture and
walls and art and blankets
and everything around me—

J

Dear Jack—

your hands.

where

where are your hands.

Jillian

Dear Jack—

Sometimes there are messages

messages on my answering machine

and these messages are music

music and nothing but music

and I'm wondering, is that

you, Jack? Is that you?

Jill

Dear Jack

I feel tense

sometimes I say too much

sometimes I say not enough

sometimes, in fear of saying
not enough, I say too much

sometimes I worry about these things

J

Dear Jack—

What

is a happy ending

J

Dear Jack—

I want you
for my pupil.

I will teach you.

I know
many things.

Dear Jack—

I remember watching
your lips, teeth

your mouth move and
your face

as you spoke
from across the room

and I sat, perched and thinking
what a surprisingly sexy

mouth
you have

J—

Dear Jack—

can you stand it

if I shine

Dear Jack—

rub my skin with salts and oils
anoint me with your touch your hands

Dear Jack—

when you were much
much younger did your
eyes shine that way
anyway? I bet they
did. I bet they
            do.

Dear Jack,

my solitude

comforts

Jill

jack—

nothing

—jill

Dear Jack—

The Queen of Hearts.

Jill

if I had more skin
I'd touch you with it

Hey Jill—
where's
Jack?

you
tell
me

Dear Jack—

my pillow misses the impression of your head

my hip remembers the curve of your palm

my eyes rest on memories of your shoulder, chest, thigh—

my arms, to hold you—

Jillian

Dear Jack—

so I said
what I said

and what
happens next

follows

love

Jill

Dear Jack—

out walking the dog, nearly
nauseous, not enough sleep last
night, dog woke me at 6 this a.m.,
loud loud bark bark nearby caterwauling
trailing off then there was the garbage
pick up and then recycling or maybe
recycling thieves bark bark bark
it's as if she saves it all up all
day long several days barely even
a single sound except her joyous sounds,
those yawny-yeowly sounds that
sometimes sound like "mama" but
barely does she ever bark and then,
and then, rapid fire.

I want your touch.

Jill

Dear Jack—

think of you
think of you
think of you

and every day happens
as it happens
anyway

J.

Jacques—

learned some french in the car
this weekend. a tape. à droit.
à gauche. à tout droit.

l'oiseau,
Jill

Jack—

no language to reach you

J—

in my mind, your hand
reaches to touch my face

moves across my eyes
wiping them away

J

Dear Jack—

the book too.
how can this be.

you barely began
to exist

and then
everything

Dear Jack—

I'm going out for a while.

I know you don't mind.

Jill

dear Jack—

each little syllable
offering

a chance to be profound

grains of sand—
and fingers

Jillian

Dear Jack—

unanswered
phone calls et cetera

have to find another
object of attention object
of affection object of desire

Jill

I cannot think of never
can only think of if

how will you know
I think of you
so much

what is this
to be "over" someone
like a sickness or
a rash

Dear Jack—

last night I drank too much
wine
this is a poem about
alcohol
and longing

J—

a kiss

to yearn

Dear Jack—

a fine man.
attractive. very attractive.
much to admire. many qualities.

hurtful intentions—
not one. not one.

with love,
Jillian

Dear Jack—

you're all Jack to me

Jill

how will you know
I think
so much

Dear Jack—

I am almost done with this
notebook. Will I then
be done with you?

love,
Jill

Dear Jack—

a page with purple grid
lines on white

I want to say "waiting to be filled" but
I don't believe it. A notebook doesn't
wait for anything: it simply is.

What qualities have I mistakenly
attributed to you?

Dear Jack—

the blank page   a page
of possibilities

each word changes
erodes
multiplies
and et cetera

Jillian

Dear Jack—

I want your tongue

Dear Jack—

an afternoon walk, somewhere
San Francisco setting:

coffee, or tea

never me

Regrets,
regards—

Jillian

Dear Jack—
some of us
have to work
you know—

Jill

Dear Jack—

Do you mind
if I kiss you

before bed tonight?
I pucker, know air

Reach for your hand
touch pillow, blanket

close eyes tight
to dream of you

Jillian

Dear Jack—

An Island

A Sea

coexisting

to join destroys the island
but what then of the sea

sandier than ever

and

and

Jill

Dear Jack—

now that I know how
tender you really are

I feel like you're
making love with me
all the time

I don't even
need you

to touch me

Jillian

The clouds look like
fire outside.

It is dark.
I am burning.

Dear Jack—

I've got it bad

can't sleep
can't sleep
can't sleep
can't sleep

Jill

no relief
not even a dream

it's not that I want
to run away from

it's that I want to
run to

what am I to do—
there is only one of me
and yet I want to do
everything—

and sometimes nothing at all

how to be—how to be—

so many choices

Dear Jack—

the long view
from the hill
near the Palace
by Clement, through
the neighborhoods, downtown,
to the Bay,
the hills and
hills behind—

and where
do you
fit
in all
this

Jill

Dear Jack—

have you ever
made love
to someone
and thought
of someone
else

or something
else

or nothing

Jill

Dear Jack—

A book filled

What happens next

Jill

Dear Jack—

do my words touch you

with love

Jill

Dear Jack,

The pen, more familiar
than any part of your body

The song of language
more known than your love
sounds, smooth sheets of paper
I can touch when I desire

Where does thought end and
imagination begin where do I
end and you begin where
are your hands, your hands
and when will they hold
these pages, this body—

       —come,
let me tell you a
story, lie with me

Jill

Dear Jack—

I thought I was through
with you I was wrong

Jill

Dear Jack—

if I drink a lot an awful
lot I will forget you
(at least around the edges)

until I reread these words
and then you'll be back

to remind me of your absence

Dear Jack—

Adore me.
I want you to adore me.

Jillian

Dear Jack—

tumbled
smooth
polished

all rough edges gone

why would I
choose
this

love

Jill—

Dear Jack—

left you

a sentence

never received
your word

love

Jill

Dear Jack—

I want to tell you
something

listen

with love

Jill